THE GLOBE THEATRE
IS PROUD TO PRESENT A NEW SEASON OF
Mr. William Shakespeare's Plays

As You Like It Come along to the magical Forest of Arden for this romantic comedy. Join in the love and laughter. **Page 6**

Antony and Cleopatra Witness what happens when Rome's greatest general falls for Egypt's powerful and beautiful queen. **Page 10**

Richard III The tale of a man so twisted by fate and ambition, his very breath is evil! **Page 16**

Twelfth Night Be confused and amused as the mythical land of Illyria plays host to shipwrecked twins. **Page 20**

King Lear Perhaps the saddest of all Will's tragedies. A family saga to make you weep. **Page 24**

The Merchant of Venice A romantic comedy entwined with tragedy. Will you dare lend or borrow money again? **Page 30**

Much Ado About Nothing Can you be tricked into love? What happens if you jump to conclusions? This romantic comedy will reveal all! **Page 34**

✳

There are three parts to each performance:
the words that Shakespeare actually wrote are those spoken by the actors;
the plot of the play is told underneath the pictures; and around the stage
stand the rude and noisy spectators.

Seats at bargain prices!
Courtyard: 1p ✳ Gallery: 2p ✳ Cushions: 3p

THE FLAG WILL FLY AND THE TRUMPET SOUND ONE HOUR
BEFORE EACH PERFORMANCE.

The audience is asked to refrain from throwing hard objects
at the performers. Rotten fruit and veg only, please.
BEWARE OF PICKPOCKETS!

✳

Long live our gracious Queen Elizabeth I!

For Ella
with love and merriment

First published 2000 by Walker Books Ltd
87 Vauxhall Walk, London SE11 5HJ

2 4 6 8 10 9 7 5 3 1

© 2000 Marcia Williams

This book has been typeset in
Monotype Centaur and Truesdell.

Printed in Italy

British Library Cataloguing in Publication Data
A catalogue record for this book is available
from the British Library.

ISBN 0-7445-6793-9

Bravo, Mr. William SHAKESPEARE!

PRESENTED
AND ILLUSTRATED BY

Marcia Williams

WALKER BOOKS
AND SUBSIDIARIES
LONDON · BOSTON · SYDNEY

AS YOU LIKE IT

Alas!

Many summers ago, in France, Duke Frederick's court was enjoying a day of wrestling. The fearsome giant, Monsieur Charles, was taking on all comers. Only Rosalind, Frederick's niece, was sad. She was pining for her father, the rightful duke, whom Frederick had banished to the Forest of Arden after stealing his crown.

I pray thee, Rosalind, sweet my coz, be merry.

Neither her dear cousin, Celia, nor Touchstone, the jester, could comfort Rosalind.

Give over this attempt.

Do, young sir.

And now Orlando, to whom Rosalind had taken a fancy, was going to fight Monsieur Charles.

The little strength that I have, I would it were with you.

Orlando had also fallen for Rosalind, so he wanted to prove his strength.

Yo! Yo! Orlando.

Orlando was strong indeed! Everyone watched in awe as he skilfully floored the giant.

I would thou hadst told me of another father.

Even Frederick cheered, until he learned Orlando's father had been his enemy.

I do in friendship counsel you to leave this place.

Wear this for me.

A courtier urged Orlando to leave court. Rosalind sadly gave her love a parting gift.

Ooh, Ducky, it's love!

He's a real tyrant.

Mistress, dispatch you with your safest haste, And get you from our court.

If she be a traitor, why so am I.

But Frederick then threw Rosalind from court. Celia, his daughter, was shocked. She resolved to leave too, and help Rosalind find her father.

Call me Ganymede.

No longer Celia, but Aliena.

They decided to travel to the Forest of Arden in disguise, Rosalind as the poor youth, "Ganymede", and Celia as his sister, "Aliena".

They are brave going to the forest!

It's not scary.

Takes one to know one!

Ooh, the old imposter!

Throw a rat at him!

Want to buy an orange for the journey?

Don't be daft, they need ale!

Is the jest going too

Cock-a-doodle-doo!   Tweet!   Tweet!

Blow, blow thou winter wind,
Thou art not so unkind
As man's ingratitude...

Why, what's the matter?

He means to burn the lodging where you lie. Do not enter.

Orlando returned to the home he shared with his older brother, Oliver. Adam, an elderly servant, greeted him with bad news.

What! Would'st thou have me go and beg my food?

I have five hundred crowns... Let me go with you.

Oliver, who had always been jealous of Orlando, planned to murder him. Orlando fled with Adam to the Forest of Arden.

Find out thy brother wheresoe'er he is. Seek him with candle; bring him dead or living...

I never lov'd my brother in my life.

When Duke Frederick heard that Orlando and Adam had fled to Arden too, he hoped they might lead him to his beloved daughter, Celia. He sent for Oliver and ordered him to go and look for Orlando in the forest.

O Jupiter! How weary are my spirits.

I care not for my spirits, if my legs were not weary.

I pray you, bear with me: I cannot go no further.

In the meantime, "Ganymede", "Aliena" and their companion, Touchstone, had reached the forest. They felt exhausted and afraid.

I like this place.

Bring us where we may rest ourselves.

FOR SALE

A kind shepherd helped them find food and shelter, so they could rest before beginning their search for Rosalind's father.

I almost die for food; and let me have it.

Sit down and feed, and welcome to our table.

**All the world's a stage,
And all the men and women merely players:
They have their exits and their entrances;
And one man in his time plays many parts,
His acts being seven ages.**

When Orlando and Adam reached the forest, they too felt tired and hungry, especially the aged Adam. Fortunately, they came across the deposed duke's camp where they were made welcome. As Adam revived, one of the duke's courtiers, Jaques, entertained them with a long speech.

Left margin:

You'll never make a cock!

Why waste a good candle on a brother!

They're just not used to being peasants.

Peasants aren't used to being peasants!

That Orlando should put his sword away and say please!

Right margin:

Send for Will. We wish to praise him.

Will's with the groundlings, Majesty.

Hey, Will! What's them seven acts got to do with this plot?

Bottom margin:

Are you collecting for us poor?

Is that Robin Hood?

No, pet, that's the real duke.

Ask if he's got a quill handy for an autograph...

Not a lot, but it's a great speech!

In the mysterious, magical Forest of Arden, strange things began to happen. Touchstone the jester fell for Audrey, a goatherd. Phebe, a shepherdess, fell for "Ganymede", making her sweetheart, Silvius, sad. Orlando professed his love for Rosalind to "Ganymede", who dared not reveal her disguise. Only "Aliena" was without an admirer.

Then one day in the forest, Orlando found a lion and a snake about to attack a sleeping man.

The snake vanished when it saw Orlando, but the lion prepared to pounce.

Orlando realized the man was Oliver, his brother. He slew the lion and saved him. Oliver felt ashamed and the brothers were reunited.

But Orlando was due to visit "Ganymede" and "Aliena". He sent Oliver ahead to explain the delay, while he bandaged a wound.

At first sight, Oliver and "Aliena" fell head over heels in love.

Oliver raced back to tell Orlando all about "Aliena".

Orlando, no stranger to instant love, bid him marry the next day.

At last, "Aliena" had found both love and a husband.

8

It was a lover and his lass,
With a hey, and a ho, and a hey nonino.

That o'er the green corn-field did pass,
In the spring time, the only pretty ring time,
When birds do sing, hey ding a ding, ding...

I am a magician.

You will have her when I bring her? That would I.

You will bestow Rosalind on Orlando? That would I.

From hence I go.

Hey. Ding. Ding. Ding. Ding.

THE BLACK-FRIARS BOYS

Thanks to "Ganymede", the wedding did not go quite as expected.

First, she made Orlando vow to marry Rosalind if she could find her.

Then she made her father, the duke, vow to give Rosalind away.

Finally, "Ganymede" vanished with the bride, "Aliena".

I love a happy ending!

But what will happen when they leave the forest?

You're bloomin' gloom and doom.

Verily, a merry play!

I love it when Will goes daft!

Can I touch the fairies?

No, they're moths!

What's a Greek god doing here?

Truly, it makes you want to dance!

When they reappeared, the girls were dressed once more as Rosalind and Celia. Hymen, the god of marriage, attended them. The duke was overjoyed, and Orlando and Oliver embraced their transformed lovers. When Phebe saw that "Ganymede" was a girl, she at last fell in love with Silvius. Touchstone and Audrey skipped with delight. In the midst of all this joy, a messenger came from Frederick to say he repented of his wicked ways and wished to return the crown to his brother, the rightful duke. After Hymen had blessed the happy couples, everyone sang and danced for one last day in the mysterious Forest of Arden.

A verily merrily play, I say!

Verily, verily, merrily, merrily...

Too good to be true, I say!

Don't be daft, it's a play.

Are you allowed?

Nay!

Get this ass out of here.

When are you leavin' then?

ANTONY AND CLEOPATRA

83BC MARK ANTONY 31BC 63BC OCTAVIUS CAESAR 14AD 89BC AEMILIUS LEPIDUS 12BC

Three men, Mark Antony, young Octavius Caesar and Aemilius Lepidus once ruled the Roman world. Caesar and Lepidus took care of the affairs of state in Italy, but Antony made merry in Egypt.

If it be love indeed, tell me how much.

Antony was in love with Egypt's queen, Cleopatra, and could not bear to leave her.

News, my good lord, from Rome. *Grates me; the sum.* *Nay, hear them, Antony.*

But news came that his wife, Fulvia, had died and his power in Rome was weakening.

I must with haste from hence. *Why, then, we kill all our women.* *I am sick and sullen.*

In spite of Cleopatra's pleas, Antony and his good friend, Enobarbus, left for Rome.

He fishes, drinks, and wastes the lamps of night in revel. *I must not think there are evils enough to darken all his goodness.*

Caesar and Lepidus resented the time the once noble Antony spent in Egypt, and despised his neglect of duty.

A sister I bequeath you, whom no brother did ever love so dearly; let her live to join our kingdoms and our hearts. *Happily, amen!* *The world and my great office will sometimes divide me from your bosom.*

In order to strengthen his alliance with the two leaders once more, Antony agreed to marry Caesar's sister, Octavia.

You have made me offer of Sicily, Sardinia; and I must rid all the sea of pirates. *That's our offer.* *Give's your hand.* *O, Antony!* *Pompey, good night.*

Next, the three rulers set about retrieving their strength at sea, which another powerful Roman general, Sextus Pompey, had usurped during Antony's long absence. A peace treaty was signed and Antony celebrated late into the night with his old friend, Pompey.

The Globe

I hope that lion isn't real!

Just like Julius. Ruthless ambition.

Shame you're not a relative.

Hop-along-rabbit for sale! Fresh or cooked!

Hop off!

Hey, Antony, if you're leaving can I have her?

That poor Octavia. He'll never leave Cleo.

Squirrel for sale! Nice tasty squirrel!

How can we follow the plot with you rabbiting on? *What plot?* *I love a good plot.* *You want that Marlowe fellow.* *And you want the exit, you crusty botch!*

10

Hey, Eno, he'll cry all right when he hears my farewell music!

Farewell, my dearest sister.
Will Caesar weep?
My noble brother!
Let all the number of the stars give light to thy fair way!

Spoke scantly of me.
O my good lord! Believe not all.

Yourself shall go between's.
Thanks to my lord.

The eagle has landed.

Antony felt he had now done everything he could to retain his position. He left for Athens with Octavia.

But before long, news reached Athens that Caesar had killed Pompey, imprisoned Lepidus and publicly scorned Antony.

Only Octavia might be able to prevent a war between her husband and brother. She left for Rome at once.

Compared to some, that's all she is!

But you are come a market-maid to Rome.
To come thus was I not constrain'd, but did it on my free-will.

God's bread! Is there to be no music!

Cleopatra hath nodded him to her.
Ay me, most wretched.

Octavia chose to travel the distance without ceremony, but her modest arrival infuriated Caesar. He felt Antony had insulted his sister.

Then came the news that, in Octavia's absence, Antony had gone to see Cleopatra in Egypt. War between the two leaders was inevitable.

Good, good! Trouble ahead - war and gore.

He's married, madam.
Rogue! Thou hast liv'd too long.

When Cleopatra had heard the news of Antony's marriage to Octavia she had nearly murdered the messenger in a jealous fury. But when Antony came back to her, she welcomed him with open arms.

You used to be noble, Ant. What happened?

Ask his mum.

We will fight with him by sea.
By sea! What else?

Your ships are not well mann'd. Their ships are yare; yours, heavy.
I'll fight at sea.

I have sixty sails, Caesar, none better.
By sea, by sea.

The reunited lovers decided to fight Caesar at sea, their galleys sailing together.

Enobarbus begged Antony not to fight at sea. Antony was better at fighting on land.

But Antony had ears only for Cleopatra. They left for their ships, side by side.

some 'as kids, and some 'as fleas.
Well I know whom I'd rather be next to.
Verily, love is making you stupid.
Don't do it, Ant!
Yo, Caesar!
Pish to Caesar.

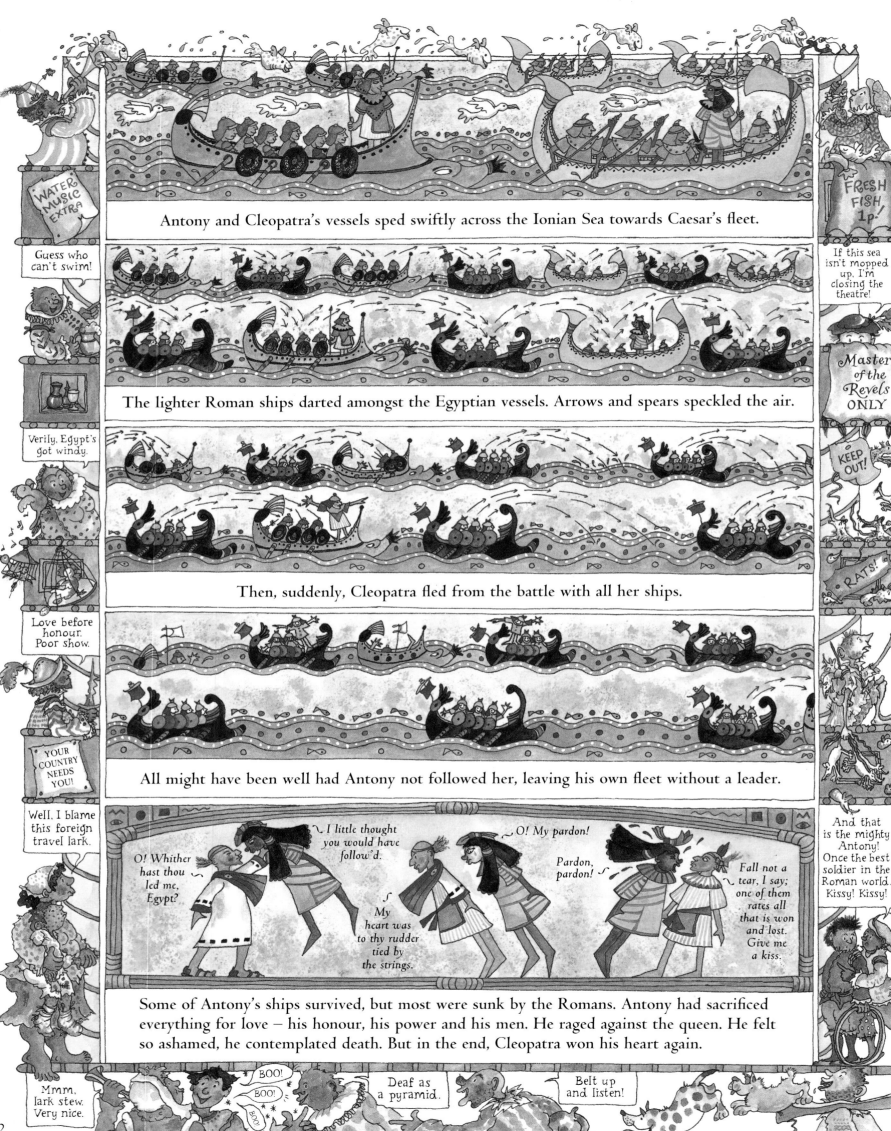

Antony and Cleopatra's vessels sped swiftly across the Ionian Sea towards Caesar's fleet.

The lighter Roman ships darted amongst the Egyptian vessels. Arrows and spears speckled the air.

Then, suddenly, Cleopatra fled from the battle with all her ships.

All might have been well had Antony not followed her, leaving his own fleet without a leader.

Some of Antony's ships survived, but most were sunk by the Romans. Antony had sacrificed everything for love – his honour, his power and his men. He raged against the queen. He felt so ashamed, he contemplated death. But in the end, Cleopatra won his heart again.

Antony and Cleopatra sent a messenger to Rome to offer Caesar terms for peace. But Caesar would not forgive Antony. And he sent word that he would make peace with Cleopatra only if she drove Antony from Egypt, or had him killed.

Caesar also sent a cunning soldier, Thyreus, to try to win Cleopatra from Antony.

When Antony saw Thyreus kiss Cleopatra's hand he suspected her of treachery.

Once more Cleopatra soothed Antony's anger. He decided to fight on against Caesar.

Much of Antony's army had deserted. Now Enobarbus left.

It was with a heavy heart that Antony went into battle.

Yet the victory that day went to him.

Cleopatra and Antony celebrated all through the night.

The following day the battle moved from land to sea and Antony manned Cleopatra's galleys with his best troops. Once more, Antony seemed assured of victory. But then, without warning, Cleopatra's boats yielded again to Caesar.

This time Antony was certain that Cleopatra had betrayed him. He wanted her to die.

Cleopatra took refuge in her tomb and sent word to Antony that she had killed herself.

Antony's rage turned to despair. All was lost now – his honour, his power, his beloved Cleopatra.

Left without hope, Antony ordered his faithful servant, Eros, to kill him.

To avoid the pain of killing his master, Eros turned his sword upon himself.

So Antony fell upon his own sword. Although the wound was fatal, his life lingered on.

As he lay dying, a servant came from Cleopatra to say the queen still lived. Antony begged to be carried to her tomb.

Fearing Caesar's vengeful arrival, Cleopatra would not leave her tomb. Antony was hauled aloft and died in her arms.

Caesar was determined to capture Cleopatra alive as a symbol of his victory.

He sent Proculeius to the tomb to prevent the queen from following her lover.

Proculeius entered the tomb just in time to stop Cleopatra from stabbing herself.

It's too flippin' cold being Egyptian.

Our care and pity is so much upon you, that we remain your friend.

He words me, girls, he words me.

Show me, my women, like a queen... Bring our crown and all.

Weirder and weirder, Will!

Then Caesar himself arrived. While pretending to be Cleopatra's friend, he secretly plotted to parade her as his prisoner through Rome.

Cleopatra was not deceived by Caesar. She ordered her maids, Charmian and Iras, to fetch her finest robes.

Cleo, lovey, before you die, can I be in your next play?

Hast thou the pretty worm of Nilus there?

Dost thou not see my baby at my breast, that sucks the nurse asleep?

O Antony!

Get those wriggling creatures out of here, verily.

Then the guard allowed a farmer to deliver a basket of figs.

Hidden in the basket were two poisonous asps.

Cleopatra put one serpent to her breast, and one to her arm.

As the asps delivered their venom, Cleopatra thought of Antony.

Sadly I am not able to clap.

In death Antony and Cleopatra had outwitted Caesar and robbed him of his triumph. Yet Antony had once been the noblest of Roman generals and, in spite of their quarrels, Caesar mourned for him. Now he ordered that the bodies of Charmian and Iras, who had also died by poison, be removed from the monument. His army then attended Antony and Cleopatra's funeral with full solemnity, placing the two lovers together in the queen's tomb. They would stay in death as they had in life, side by side.

Call that acting?

Just lying around in boxes!

It's the deadliest curtain call I've ever seen.

They're mummies, you dummies!

That was awesome!

The Tragedy of KING RICHARD III

Since I cannot prove a lover, to entertain these fair well-spoken days, I am determined to prove a villain.

In 1483, King Edward IV of England lay close to death. His son, the Prince of Wales, would inherit the crown even though he was still a child. The boy's uncle, hunchbacked Richard, Duke of Gloucester, had been made "Lord Protector" of the realm, and entrusted with the prince's care. But really Richard wanted the crown himself. And he was ready to use any means to get it, however foul…

I feel a bit of intrigue coming on.

Foul devil. — *Lady, you know no rules of charity.*

Out of my sight! Thou dost infect mine eyes. — *Thine eyes, sweet lady, have infected mine.*

Though I wish thy death, I will not be thy executioner. — *Vouchsafe to wear this ring.*

How does he get away with it?

Richard knew a king should have a well-born wife. He decided to court Anne, a royal widow. Since Richard himself had killed her husband and her father-in-law, Anne was disgusted when he came to woo her at the funeral. But the wily Richard talked so cleverly he won her round.

Family loyalty! I love it.

His majesty … hath appointed This conduct to convey me to the Tower. — *I will deliver you.*

Who'd kill for a crown?

Elizabeth E. R.

Richard also needed to be rid of his older brother, the popular Duke of Clarence. He persuaded the weakening King Edward to imprison him as a traitor in the terrible Tower of London. The unsuspecting Clarence loved Richard and trusted him to secure his release.

Shall we stab him as he sleeps? — *No; he'll say 'twas done cowardly, when he wakes.*

I will send you to my brother Gloucester. — *Your brother Gloucester hates you.*

Relent and save your souls. — *Relent! 'Tis cowardly.*

If all this will not do, I'll drown you in the malmsey-butt within.

Not in my butt you don't!

Instead, Richard hired a pair of assassins to murder Clarence in his cell.

Verily, 'tis hard to believe such wickedness.

Methinks Richard's pockets would be rich pickings.

Rich in evil!

Aah, "To sleep: perchance to dream…" Now who said that?

Madam, bethink you, like a careful mother, of the young prince your son: send straight for him; let him be crown'd.

My lord … let not us two stay at home.

My other self … my oracle, my prophet!

Soon King Edward died. His widow, Queen Elizabeth — well aware of Richard's ambition — quickly sent her brothers to bring the Prince of Wales back to London for his coronation.

But Richard and his sly friend, the Duke of Buckingham, pursued them.

Sanctuary won't save you. Flee the country.

Come, come, my boy; we will to sanctuary.

I'll conduct you to the sanctuary.

I shall not sleep in quiet at the Tower.

I fear no Uncles dead.

Nor none that live, I hope.

You'll sleep quiet. He'll see to that.

When Elizabeth heard Richard had taken her eldest son and imprisoned her brothers, she was scared. She fled with her second son, the young Duke of York, and sought holy sanctuary.

But Richard had no respect for holy sanctuary, and ordered little York to be taken from his mother. Then he locked the two young princes in the Tower, safely out of the way.

Unwise words, sirrah!

I'll have this crown of mine cut from my shoulders Before I'll see the crown so foul misplac'd.

Look how I am bewitch'd; behold mine arm…

Thou protector of this damned strumpet!

Off with his head!

O bloody Richard! Miserable England!

Chip-chop! Many a true word…

By now Hastings, the Lord Chamberlain, had guessed Richard's plans.

So Richard falsely accused Queen Elizabeth of witchcraft.

He knew Hastings would never sign her death warrant.

He then declared Hastings a traitor and had him beheaded.

I warrant they won't be joyful for long!

Good my lord; your citizens entreat you.

Refuse not, mighty lord.

O! Make them joyful.

Ha! Am I king? 'Tis so: but… I wish the bastards dead.

Could he kill the little princes?

Next, Buckingham spread rumours that the royal princes had been born out of wedlock. Soon the people began to call for Richard to be king.

The villain had succeeded! He was crowned King Richard III of England. But he did not feel safe while the little princes still lived.

Break out the rotten eggs!

But don't hit Hastings.

Give us some.

So the killing doesn't end here?

Now, do you dare turn the page?

One breath and you're dead, Buck!

1593

Methinks these tidings are not welcome.

Hastings' head! A penny a peek!

Say, have I thy consent that they shall die?

Give me some little breath.

But his friend Buckingham was reluctant to kill the children.

Dar'st thou resolve to kill a friend of mine?

Please you; but I had rather kill two enemies.

So Richard paid an assassin to smother the boys as they slept.

My lord, I claim the gift, my due by promise.

I am not in the giving vein today.

Angry with Buckingham, Richard refused him a long-promised earldom.

Made I him king for this? O, let me think on Hastings, and be gone ... while my fearful head is on.

Buckingham fled to join the growing forces against the king.

Headless is all the rage...

1593

That's a weight off his hump.

Richmond aims at young Elizabeth, my brother's daughter, and, by that knot, looks proudly on the crown.

Richard believed he could be secure only if he got rid of Anne and married the dead princes' sister, Elizabeth. But news came that Henry, Earl of Richmond, was marching against him.

My liege, the Duke of Buckingham is taken.

Richard knew he must fight Richmond or lose the crown. He rallied his army and set out for Wales. Along the way he was delighted to hear that his men had captured Buckingham.

I've a hunch things are not going to end happily!

Let thy soul despair.

Despair and die!

Despair and die!

Despair and die!

Despair and die!

Despair and die!

Live, and flourish!

Awake, and win the day!

Live, and flourish!

Be cheerful.

Win the day.

The armies met on Bosworth Field. The night before battle began, both the king and Richmond dreamed of Richard's victims. One by one, the spectres wished Richard ill and the earl well.

Some people will do anything to make money.

It's tasteless. You mean it's headless!

Adults only, boy.

Is anyone watching the play?

18

A horse! A horse! My kingdom for a horse!

Good old Will! He never stints on blood and gore.

1564

...auditioned to be a soldier but, "No, not today, thanks..."

NO MUSIC WILL BE PLAYED IN THE BATTLE SCENE

Bleeding bodies everywhere. I'll close this theatre down!

Master of the Revels ONLY

Blackfriars only 1p! Avoid the bridge! Avoid the crowds! Avoid your neighbours! Take the ferry! Boat leaves in ten minutes!

The day dawned sunless and cold. Soon the field was loud with the noise of battle. Richard's side suffered heavy losses. Then his own horse was slain beneath him. But he fought on bravely until he met Richmond. The raging hunchback was no match for the earl. With one victorious stroke Richmond slew him. Richard III's short and bloody reign was over. Few mourned its passing and many celebrated the crowning of Richmond as King Henry VII. Henry then married the princes' sister, Elizabeth – uniting her house, of York, and his, of Lancaster, to bring peace to England.

Well you look dead already.

You'd have to be brain dead to fight for Richard.

33

Being a groundling is a pain in the neck!

Your grandfather fought at the battle of Bosworth.

Was he an actor then?

TWELFTH NIGHT;
or, What You Will

On a stormy night off the rocky coast of Illyria, a ship was wrecked. One of the few survivors was a gentlewoman named Viola. Her beloved twin brother, Sebastian, had vanished in the waves and Viola feared he was drowned. The ship's captain advised Viola to dress as a man and seek work at the court of Illyria's ruler, Duke Orsino.

His eyes must be blinded by tears.

I have unclasp'd to thee the book even of my secret soul.

Duke Orsino employed Viola as his page. Soon he came to trust her above all others.

Unfold the passion of my love.

I'll do my best to woo your lady.

He told her that he loved a countess called Olivia, and asked her to deliver messages of love. Viola did not relish the task for she had fallen in love with Orsino herself. But she agreed to go.

You've left out, "If music be the food of love, play on."

BOOK HOLDER'S BOX NO ENTRY SILENCE

Is all Illyria blind?

Madam, yond young fellow swears he will speak with you.

I told him you were sick.

I told him you were asleep.

Let him approach.

Olivia was in mourning for her dead brother and allowed no men into her house. But Orsino's page would not be turned away, even by Olivia's rude steward, Malvolio.

I cannot love him.

Olivia explained to Viola that she did not love his master and never would.

Methinks she's smitten by the page!

Verily, I think they are all blind.

How now! Even so quickly may one catch the plague?

But Orsino's page talked so eloquently of love that Olivia began to fall in love with *him!*

Hie thee, Malvolio.

When Viola left, Olivia sent Malvolio after the handsome page with a ring.

Poor lady, she were better love a dream.

Realizing what must have happened, Viola wished she could reveal her disguise.

"But love is blind, and lovers cannot see..."

If she finds out now, there's no plot.

A plague o' these pickled herring.

How now, sot.

Swabber!

Another eternal truth, my sweet Will.

Did I not say that?

THE GLOBE TROTTERS

"O mistress mine! Where are you roaming? O! Stay and hear; your true love's coming."

A mellifluous voice.

Have you no wit, manners, nor honesty?

They do you notorious wrong, M.

That night, Olivia went to bed. But her maid, Maria; her jester, Feste; her uncle, Sir Toby Belch and his friend, Sir Andrew Aguecheek (who Sir Toby hoped might marry Olivia), stayed up late, revelling and drinking. Suddenly, Malvolio burst in and rudely packed them off to bed.

BACON BANNED BY ORDER OF WILL AND THE TROTTERS

Blinkin' bees!

This wins him, liver and all.

This is my lady's hand!

"Remember who commended thy yellow stockings."

"Thy smile becomes thee well."

I will smile: I will do everything that thou wilt have me.

I'd have made a lovely Malvolio...

Next day, the angry revellers decided to pay Malvolio back. They dropped a letter in his path, written by Maria in Olivia's handwriting. If Malvolio would only smile and wear yellow, cross-gartered stockings, the letter said, Olivia might marry him.

"Some are born great—"

Ha!

"Some achieve greatness—"

Heaven restore thee!

"Thy yellow stockings."

Thy yellow stockings!

"Cross-gartered."

Why, this is very midsummer madness.

Is it Twelfth Night or Midsummer?

It's What You Will!

'm not what I am either! 'm a princess waiting for my prince.

Of course, when Malvolio did smile and strut his yellow stockings at her, Olivia thought he had gone mad. He quoted whole sentences from the letter, but still she looked bewildered. Finally, she gave orders that he be locked up in a dark room till he recovered.

Cluck!

I come to whet your gentle thoughts on his behalf.

Later Viola arrived. She was still acting as Orsino's page.

I love thee so.

I am not what I am.

Again Olivia rejected Orsino. She wanted to wed his page.

Yet come again.

Olivia begged the horrified page not to leave her.

I saw your niece do more favours to the count's serving-man than ever she bestowed upon me.

Challenge ... the count's youth to fight.

Sir Andrew angrily decided to challenge this new rival to a duel.

Whose play are you living in?

Jellied eels for sale! Thames-fresh!

Don't dally with an eel. Munch my mutton.

Meagre mutton morsel, mate!

Meanwhile, Antonio, an old enemy of Orsino's, had saved Sebastian, Viola's twin. Antonio lent Sebastian his purse and went looking for lodgings.

But half an hour later Antonio saw Sebastian again. In fact it was Viola, duelling with Sir Andrew. Antonio rushed to "Sebastian's" defence.

Unluckily, some soldiers recognized Antonio as the duke's enemy and arrested him.

Antonio asked "Sebastian" to buy his freedom. But Viola was astonished and refused.

Then she guessed that this man must know her brother. He must still be alive!

But Sir Andrew still wanted his duel. He and Toby chased Viola, and caught – Sebastian.

Luckily, Olivia came by. Mistaking Sebastian for Viola as well, she rescued him.

While he was still in a daze, Olivia rushed Sebastian off to be married.

Afterwards, the confused but happy Sebastian insisted on leaving his new bride while he returned Antonio's purse.

At the same time, Duke Orsino (who knew nothing of the wedding) set out with Viola to woo Countess Olivia once more.

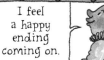

On their way, they met Antonio, who complained that the duke's page had his purse. Then up hobbled Sir Toby and Sir Andrew complaining that the duke's page had wounded them. Then, to both the duke's and Viola's horror, Olivia arrived greeting Viola as "husband"!

Then, suddenly, another Viola appeared. It seemed the page had a twin brother.

As Viola embraced Sebastian and explained she was his sister, the confusion cleared…

Duke Orsino was so amazed, he gave up his wasted love for Olivia and offered his heart to Viola, the woman who had been his page. Antonio was pardoned and got his purse back. And Olivia and Sebastian were happily reunited. As Olivia's jester, Feste, began to sing a song of celebration, everyone, except the yellow-stockinged Malvolio, linked arms in love and friendship. The terrible shipwreck on Illyria's shores had turned out to be a stroke of great good fortune.

KING LEAR

Which of you shall we say doth love us most?

In ancient Britain, the elderly King Lear decided to give up his power and divide his kingdom among his three daughters. He planned to give the largest territory to the daughter who professed to love him most. Lear was sure this would be his favourite, Cordelia.

Sir, I love you more than words can wield the matter.

The eldest, greedy Goneril of Albany, pretended to love her father very much.

She comes too short.

Lear's second daughter, Regan of Cornwall, swore she loved him even more than Goneril.

I love your majesty according to my bond; nor more nor less.

So young, and so untender?

But Cordelia, sickened by their deceit, said only that she loved him as a daughter should.

Thy truth then be thy dower.

At this, Lear flew into a rage. He disowned Cordelia and gave his lands to Goneril and Regan.

Check this hideous rashness.

Away!

When Lear's oldest friend, the Earl of Kent, tried to intervene, Lear banished him on the spot.

Thee and thy virtues here I seize upon.

But Cordelia's suitor, the King of France, admired her honesty, and asked her to marry him.

The jewels of our father, with wash'd eyes Cordelia leaves you.

Cordelia prepared to sail for France, reluctantly leaving her father in the care of her cunning sisters, Goneril and Regan.

Service.

But Kent did not leave. He disguised himself and took a job as Lear's servant, hoping to protect him from his scheming daughters.

Thou liest, thou dost not!

Will's going to make you regret this moment.

Francey, any more like you at home?

Give an old man some warmth.

Being a virgin queen does avoid these problems.

Nutty nuts for sale!

Don't be daft – he's pre-Roman.

Verily, he don't look it!

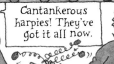

Cantankerous harpies! They've got it all now.

Men like a bit of a fuss.

Honesty doesn't pay.

Nuts!

Get these debosh'd knights away!

Here do you keep a hundred knights and squires; Men so disorder'd, so debosh'd, and bold, That this our court ... shows like a riotous inn.

How sharper than a serpent's tooth it is to have a thankless child!

DRUM LESSONS: A DUCAT A DOZEN

Lear had no palace of his own now, so he took a train of one hundred knights, his fool and his new servant to stay with Goneril. But Goneril had changed. She was no longer a loving daughter.

I have another daughter, who, I am sure, is kind and comfortable.

I'm for you, daddy Lear!

Bewildered by her harshness, Lear decided to visit Regan. He sent his servant ahead to the Earl of Gloucester's palace where she and her husband were staying. He, his knights and his fool, followed, galloping through the night.

And dads put fidgets in the stocks.

They durst not do't; They could not, would not do't.

O, they durst, I know they durst!

But when they arrived, Lear was outraged to discover that Regan and Cornwall had put his servant in the stocks. Nor would they come out and greet the king.

I may not be a Lear, but...

What need you five-and-twenty, ten, or five?

I gave you all.

What need one?

O fool! I shall go mad!

Weeping Will I call him, he makes me bellow so.

Then Goneril arrived, and the spiteful sisters told Lear he must give up his hundred knights and live as a pauper.

Lear had no daughters left to turn to. His heart bursting with sorrow, he rushed out on to the heath in a pitiless storm.

Face it, you'll never make an actor.

He's been trying for years, poor fop.

Did you think retirement would be easy?

Drown your sorrows here!

Poor soul. He'll catch his death.

25

But Cornwall's wound proved fatal. Regan was delighted. Now she would be free to marry Gloucester's son, Edmund, whom she loved.

But Goneril loved him too. Jealous of Regan, she wrote to Edmund suggesting he kill her husband, Albany, leaving *her* free to marry him.

But then news came that Cordelia had raised a French army and landed at Dover. Reluctantly the two sisters put their battle for Edmund to one side and prepared to fight Cordelia. They marshalled their troops and set off for Dover with Albany and Edmund.

Kent had also heard the news, and set out with Lear, hoping to reunite him with Cordelia. Blind Gloucester was on his way to Dover too with Edgar who had found him lost and in pain on the heath. Outside the port the two old men met: Gloucester now eyeless, and Lear mad with misery and fatigue. As the war drums rolled, Cordelia's servants came to take Lear to the French camp.

King Lear slept through the long battle. When he awoke, Cordelia and the French had been defeated. Unaware that Edmund had issued orders for his and Cordelia's deaths, Lear rejoiced. The idea of imprisonment with Cordelia seemed like heaven compared to freedom with Goneril and Regan.

Meanwhile, Albany had discovered Goneril and Edmund's plan to kill him. He declared Edmund a traitor and ordered him to defend himself.

An armoured man challenged Edmund to fight. Goneril and Regan watched as Edmund rapidly began to lose to the stranger.

Only after he had delivered a mortal blow to Edmund, did the stranger remove his helmet and reveal himself to be Edgar.

As Edmund lay dying, Edgar told him how he had been reunited with their father, Gloucester, just before his recent death.

A servant brought news that Goneril had poisoned Regan and then, realizing Edmund would not live, had killed herself too.

Edmund was conscience-stricken at last. With his final breath he told Edgar to send a reprieve for Lear and Cordelia.

Howl, howl, howl, howl!
O! You are men of stones:
Had I your tongues and eyes,
I'd use them so that heaven's
vaults should crack.

But it was too late. Lear's dear Cordelia had been hanged. Albany and Edgar watched in horror as Lear stumbled towards them carrying her body in his arms.

This play will certainly keep the gravedigger in work.

Wise words, but a bit late.

The weight of this sad time
we must obey;
Speak what we feel, not what
we ought to say.

Shall I be queen now?

Wise words always come too bloomin' late.

Beside himself with grief, the old king fell into a faint. Edgar tried to help, but Kent stopped him. Lear had lost everything. What he had not given away had been taken from him. Even his fool had been executed. Kent, who had stayed by the king's side throughout his torments, knew Lear no longer had any hope of finding peace in this world. It was with relief that he watched his friend's life gently ebb from him, his arms about his only true daughter, Cordelia. Albany tried to persuade Kent to take the crown, but the old earl had no use for life without Lear. So Edgar became king and tried to rule with honour, in memory of two wronged old men: his father, the Earl of Gloucester, and his liege, King Lear.

Kent for King!

No, he's after following Lear.

The wife's pies for sale, or even the wife.

Watch it, you!

You won't treat your old Dad like that?

A pox on all this sadness. Let's see if the Rose has a merrier play.

The Merchant of Venice

Bassanio, a poor nobleman from Venice, was in love with Portia, a rich heiress from the country. To travel to her estate and court her, he needed three thousand ducats. His friend, the merchant Antonio, could not help. His wealth was with his ships at sea. So they asked the Jewish money-lender, Shylock. Shylock had long hated Antonio. He agreed to lend the sum, on one condition.

If the money was not returned in three months, Antonio must pay with a pound of his flesh. Antonio rashly agreed.

Bassanio now prepared to woo Portia at her house in Belmont. His good friend, Gratiano, begged to accompany him.

Before he died, Portia's father had made three caskets — one gold, one silver, one lead. On each was a riddle. The first suitor to pick the casket that contained a portrait of his daughter would win her hand. Men had flocked from far and near to try the test. All had failed.

WHO CHOOSETH ME SHALL GAIN WHAT MANY MEN DESIRE

WHO CHOOSETH ME SHALL GET AS MUCH AS HE DESERVES

WHO CHOOSETH ME MUST GIVE AND HAZARD ALL HE HATH

Now Bassanio took his turn. Portia, who loved Bassanio as much as he loved her, watched nervously, with Nerissa, her maid, and Gratiano. Gold? Silver? Or lead? Which would Bassanio choose? At last, he turned the key in the lead casket … and found his true love's portrait!

Portia gave Bassanio a ring. He swore never to part with it.

Then Nerissa gave Gratiano a ring. They had also found love.

Amid this joy, Bassanio's friend, Lorenzo, arrived. He had eloped with Shylock's daughter, Jessica. They brought grave news from Venice.

Antonio's ships had not docked and the three months were up. Shylock was demanding his bond. Antonio's life was in danger.

The couples married in haste. Then Bassanio and Gratiano left for Venice. Portia promised enough money to pay off the debt many times over.

Left behind, Portia wrote to her cousin, a learned lawyer, Doctor Bellario. She asked him to send lawyers' clothes and books about the law.

Next Portia asked Lorenzo and Jessica to look after her house. She and Nerissa would await their husbands' return in a monastery.

When Bassanio, Gratiano and Antonio reached Belmont, they never guessed Portia and Nerissa had just returned too.

At first the wives seemed pleased to see their husbands. Then Nerissa asked Gratiano where the ring she had given him was.

Soon Bassanio was in trouble with Portia too. Both wives claimed to be offended.

But when Antonio interceded, Portia relented. She bade him pass Bassanio a ring.

Nerissa also relented and gave Gratiano a ring. It seemed familiar.

Bassanio and Gratiano realized that these were the very rings they had given away. So Portia had been the young lawyer who had saved Antonio's life, and Nerissa her clerk! How blind they had been. Then Nerissa told Jessica that even though she had eloped with Lorenzo, she would inherit Shylock's wealth when he died. And Antonio discovered that his ships with all their merchandise had finally come safely into harbour. At last the merry friends could celebrate, and laugh at the husbands who had not known their own wives!

MUCH ADO ABOUT NOTHING

In the top panel speech bubbles:
I learn in this letter that Don Pedro of Aragon comes this night to Messina.
He is very near...

In Messina, Sicily, Governor Leonato's household was expecting guests – Don Pedro, the Prince of Aragon, his brother Don John, and two young officers, Claudio and Signior Benedick. The last time these gallants visited, they had been off to war. Now, they would have time for fun.

Speech bubbles: *Count, take of me my daughter.* / *I am yours.*

On their arrival, young Claudio realized he loved Leonato's daughter, sweet Hero. He asked the governor for her hand in marriage.

Speech bubbles: *What! My dear Lady Disdain, are you yet living?* / *Is it possible Disdain should die while she hath such meet food to feed it?*

But when proud Signior Benedick met Hero's haughty cousin Beatrice once more, they fell to their old game of arguing.

Speech bubbles: *I had rather hear my dog bark at a crow than a man swear he loves me.* / *I will live a bachelor.*

Beatrice and Benedick both scorned the idea of marriage as much as they scorned one another. Each was determined to stay single.

Speech bubbles: *I will ... bring Signior Benedick and the Lady Beatrice into a mountain of affection the one with the other.* / *My lord, I am for you.* / *And I, my lord.*

But the prince, Don Pedro, thought they were well-matched. He asked Leonato, Claudio and Hero to help him trick them into marriage.

Speech bubbles: *What was it you told me of today, that your niece Beatrice was in love with Signior Benedick?* / *She loves him with an enraged affection.* / *Tears her hair, prays, curses, "O sweet Benedick!"*

The next day Benedick just happened to overhear Don Pedro, Claudio and Leonato say that Beatrice was sick for love of him.

Speech bubbles: *This can be no trick.* / *Love me!* / *It must be requited!* / *I have railed so long against marriage.* / *They say the lady is fair.* / *I did never think to marry!*

Convinced Leonato would not lie, Benedick believed them. He resolved to give up being proud and love Beatrice back.

Left margin text:
Romantic music? Or battle music?
Not if I get my hands on you!
Just you keep your enraged affection away from me!

Right margin text:
Just a little hillock would do me
Ye olde soft cushions verily only 3p hire
I did never think to marry either, but if it comes to us a...

Bottom margin text:
That enraged affection's worse than the plague!
That's right, Ducks, you move over here.
They'll close the theatre if there's plague about.
Let's get out of here - that trout's got the plague.

Later, Beatrice just happened to overhear Hero and her maid say that Benedick was sick for love of her.

Convinced her sweet cousin would not lie, Beatrice believed them. She resolved to give up being haughty and return Benedick's love.

But meanwhile, Don Pedro's spiteful brother, Don John, and his cohort, Borachio, were plotting to ruin Hero's wedding plans.

Don John took Don Pedro and Claudio to a window, where they *thought* they saw Hero embrace Borachio.

The following day, as Friar Francis was about to marry them, Claudio accused Hero of disloyalty.

When Don Pedro also bore witness against Hero, even her own father began to believe the slanderous accusation.

However, Leonato soon came to his senses when Hero fell to the ground in a death-like trance. This also gave Friar Francis an idea.

He would take Hero into hiding and then announce the false news of her death. The shock might knock some sense into Claudio.

Her cousin slandered, Beatrice asked Benedick to challenge Claudio to a duel.

But before the fight, Borachio was heard to boast of his conspiracy with Don John.

Borachio was arrested and confessed he had embraced not Hero – but a maid dressed in Hero's clothes. Don John's flight confirmed the story.

Filled with remorse, Claudio begged Leonato to punish him for having (as he believed) caused sweet Hero's death.

Leonato instructed Claudio to spend the night beside Hero's tomb, singing of her innocence.

Then, the next morning, Claudio must go to Friar Francis and marry Hero's unknown cousin. As the chapel bells rang out, two ladies arrived, each hidden behind a mask.

The first mask revealed Hero, not her unknown cousin. Claudio was overcome with joy!

The second hid Beatrice, still bent on teasing her beloved Benedick.

Did one receive an invitation?

HELP!

Come back, Drake, or I'll send you to fight the Armada!

Majesty is always welcome.

Master of the Revels ONLY

Love!

BRAVO! BRAVO!

After much playful banter, which Benedick put a stop to with a kiss, Beatrice agreed to marry him. The delighted Friar Francis united the two couples. When news arrived that Don John had been captured, the wedding party decided to think about a punishment for him another day. Today was a day to revel in their recovered happiness, to feast and dance through the sun-filled day and sweet-scented Sicilian night!

O merriment and love.

Nice one, Will!

I'm going to be an actor.

I'm going to Sicily!

Hic!